A L [barcode] E
G A Y
S A I N T S

K A Y L E B   R A E   C A N D R I L L I

Distributed by Independent Publishers Group Chicago

ALL THE GAY SAINTS

KAYLEB RAE CANDRILLI

Saturnalia Books
105 Woodside Rd.
Ardmore, PA 19003
info@saturnaliabooks.com

ISBN: 978-1-947817-12-8 (print), 978-1-947817-13-5 (ebook)
Library of Congress Control Number: 2019952591

Cover painting: Nocturne, 2016, oil on canvas, Tomas Harker
Cover and book design by Robin Vuchnich
Printing by Versa Press
Author photo by Jack Papanier

Distributed by:
Independent Publishing Group
814 N. Franklin St.
Chicago, IL 60610
800-888-4741

for jackie

all light floats

CONTENTS

WHEN I TRANSITION WILL I LOSE MY TASTE FOR THE STORM?

The woman who reads
my palms only speaks

of my eyes. This isn't unexpected.
Last week a new cloud was born

into the world atlas. Asperitas
is the wave that rises before the end

of something that looks most
like the world. In wartime

boundaries bend like my body
before an admittance.

And I'll admit, I once prayed
to undulate but now I'd prefer

to shave or skim or scalpel or sail.
I want to be soft and what

is softer than the sky
before it breaks?

ON WANTING TOP SURGERY IN THE FASCIST REGIME

It is clear that if I communicate all the ways I hurt
I will lose my usefulness. So instead, I'll say my father
put every pulse in the freezer and handed me a stethoscope.

Metaphors are made to protect the poet. My body is crown
molding, Victorian in its posture and its ability to keep secrets.
My breasts disgust me deeply but I depend on them for a reason

to cry. I remember no Januaries and I have a habit of drinking
the snow to whiskey. I am light as a feather, stiff as deep
crescent scars.   //   When I remove my breasts

will I feel a phantom suckling? A ghostly-unborn thing
that I love. I tell my partner that as a child I watched Casper
over and over again and they say this is because I am often harmless,

often a ghost. But the bottom line is I plan to rip myself apart.
The bottom line is I love being a boy and my body has never
been pastoral or believed much in walls.
                                        The bottom line is I drink
the body to solar power and I will still make a beautiful mother.

WHEN FACE TO FACE WITH FASCISM
(OR, THERE IS SO MUCH COUNTRY FOR OLD MEN, SO)

First, forget joy. Second, feel weak
        for forgetting and then remember.
                Third, buy spring

assisted knives and practice
        stabbing the grey clogged air.
                Notice that when the air

bleeds, it does bleed red,
        which is unexpected and
                reminiscent of something

almost human. I ask my neighbors
        if they love me and they
                answer in elephant tusk.

Ivory whiter than white
        gold. Teeth have nothing to do
                with a bite unless the shoe fits.

When queers love each other
        our breath is, needs to be,
                can never not be, pepper spray.

Maybe it's inappropriate
        to say that we love ourselves
                enough to kill for ourselves

but we are chanting it. I want
        to fit glitter into this poem,
                just because I need to remind

myself I'm real. So remember,
        glitter, glitter, glitter, and guns
                are real and I know I should

exercise tenderness for all
        the people that want me
                dead, but I refuse to love
                        the likes of my father.

MY SHADOW LOOKS MORE LIKE A MAN THAN I DO, SO I AM BOTH FEARFUL AND ENVIOUS

when i say i've found it difficult to access joy
i mean when light or the lack of light

multiplies my shadow
i anticipate my murder.

my murder looks like me, but much more
blue, more dirt road after rain, more moth to flame.

the sun is an empty egg.
my body is barren.

another man on the street bares his teeth
and i have never been able to discern

anger from hunger—lava from
wind in my vein.

SINNERS MUST LIVE WITH WHAT THEIR SINS SOW

During my assault, I imagine I choked
up blueish tulips and someone else's hands—

but the only thing I can conjure
in detail is the wiccan spell of protection

and my mother's recipe for wisteria.
In this life, I have grown

accustomed to rape and the need
to keep my body

a greenhouse for all
carnivorous things.

Remember: a mouth feels like it has many teeth
only when it closes.

Remember: I have built a flower
bed from a bruised

trachea, and that is only the start
of my industriousness. My skin can smell

deer pillaging the garden. My throat has turned
itself to top soil. Forget-me-

nots never stop spilling
from my neck.

THERE IS A POINT AT WHICH I TIRE OF MY OWN FEAR

//

Start with a fence,
       then peer into my chest.

A body has opened here,
       so please travel over

god quickly. God
       is a lake of blood.

The surface is often disturbed and built wholly of concentric circles.

//

Blessed are the meek for they will inherit the earth's empathy.
                                      It just may kill us all.

    A boy built on a hill can never be hidden.
    I know this because I am one.

    //

        When I meet my partner, my partner meets me
        back.   Against the wall
        we kiss and both note that today,   what breaks us
                                  is only the sun
                                  through the blinds.

                //

Queers are killed
and have always been   killed in any number
                         of ways. But my partner tells me again and again
                         how they love me, and I know one day I'll try to die

                         in their arms. I know this   is how   we will win.

                         //

MY BODY IS CONSTANTLY CONJURING A TEMPEST (OR, WEIGHING THE PROS AND CONS OF ATTENDING MY HIGH SCHOOL REUNION)

The coast of a puddle copies the way the Carolinas push
on the North Atlantic verbatim. Appalachia still means everything

to me, but I assume I could find it somewhere else if I looked.
There are a finite number of patterns in nature. Everything

has its doppelganger and nowadays I plagiarize men's
bodies indiscriminately. I have a right to take what's not mine;

this is what both men and the earth have taught me. In rural America
everyone is having an orgy in the bushes and calling it three Hail Marys.

Poached white-tailed deer film the debauchery for leverage
in the next century and I still want to mouth cruise my way through

all the boys that threatened to rape me in high school. These roads
are hot with H veins and ATVs winding through private

property. In rural America the switchbacks are built to disorient
and it is nearly impossible to be trans and alive, but here I am:

dizzy and gay and wanting to fix something I didn't break. Nowadays
I want to return home just so I might remember something good

or recognize nothing through the pine-dark. Where I grew up
I knew only one kind boy. He could build every inch

of the world with an Etch A Sketch. And I like to think
he is the only reason the ground is holding us up at all.

ON TRESPASSING

In rural America, *beware*
of dog signs are security

systems posted, point
blank in single pane

windows. The bullet always so much
worse than the bang.

Sometimes I imagine I never left
the fields in which I was unwelcome.

Sometimes I can still
see my father hiding

plywood riddled with rusty
nails under a bed of fall

leaves. In rural America
the warning is to draw

first blood. I remember
the ATVs with their popped

tires, the neighbors' horses
with their tetanused hooves.

You know, friendship
is so unlikely to bloom

where you are unwanted.
My father and the land

taught me everything
about being small and quiet.

They taught me
not to want
            a thing.

THE ONCE GIRL HUNTS TO FEED

When I was a girl
I would harvest myself

before buck season.
I would call animals

out from the forest with a mouthful
of reeds. Pastoral. Predator. It's been so long

since I was.
So please

stop judging me for all
I've killed

and instead consider the still-true
beauty of those I haven't.

My family was hungry
once. I was hungry

once. I am sorry
I opened my mouth

and I'm sorry I used it.

ON HARVESTING ONESELF

In rural America, bad
land is trans land.

And I have lived
in the fragile

space between drawn
property lines—

ownership is just
controlling both

the chisel
and the block.

What a thrill to cut
with such sure intention.

FUNERAL FOR A GIRL WHO GREW UP IN THE WOODS
(OR, AT THE ROOT)

I overdress to be outdoors. Pork pie. Right-handed buttons. Black tie slack lined down my chest. Nobody has died, but somebody has died. And I want to remember her name so I can swiss army carve it into bark, so I can say a word above her grave, set deep and bellied in an uprooted tree. White birch, genderless swatch, sloughing to pink-raw. Roots reach for sky—tongues still try to catch rain.

I know half of what it means to die slowly.
To feel specific thirst.

If this is a rural funeral, I'll turn the sunflowers to lampposts, the mountain to a procession of wrecked black cars, wet pine metallic, rubber burning. I'll turn my hands urban, my body man. My wallet will brim with opposites, a prayer card with a girl's name, psalm I'll feel in what's left of my womb. What is it to visit your own grave? To die and be more alive than ever?

I want to tell me I miss me. I want to tell me,
I'm never coming back.

IF THE WATER WEREN'T SO DEEP, NARCISSUS MIGHT NOT HAVE DROWNED (OR, WHEN COMING OUT AS TRANS TO MY YOUNGER SELF)

I live in shallow water because I refuse to learn to swim
and this is where I found you. Your hair is all reeds

and cattails and the umbilical cords of lily pads.
I will remember you as amphibious not because

that is truly who you were or what you are, but because
I am, and I need to keep loving my reflection.

We used to cut gills into each other's throats,
and then slip in love notes,

as though through the slits of school lockers.
When we read them aloud

it was only ever in my voice, the way
my tongue curves wetter than yours,

the way it swims along the reef of my teeth.
And what is a barrier anyway?

What is the difference between fresh and salt?
I don't remember anything

about you other than
the ways I still love myself.

COMFORTING MY TRANS SELF THROUGH THE NIGHT (OR, ON DREAMING MY BREASTS ARE REMOVED ONLY TO GROW BACK—AGAIN AND AGAIN)

I measure nighttime with yardsticks and scalpels.
There's such vanity in saving myself.

In my dreams, my tongue tastes of absinthe
and angel-food. Loving myself is gourmet.

Loving my trans body is running the gauntlet.
If I'm being honest, one day soon I will serve my flesh

up on a platter and hope
to live through all that blood loss.

It's dark outside
and I'd like to swallow a light bulb

so I might see inside of myself.
Really, I am just trying to live

for a while, and if this is becoming
an anthem, then: quitting is sacred.

Quitting is cutlass. Quitting is screaming
in my sleep until this body
                         plateaus.

TWO QUEERS WALKING THE BORDERLINE BETWEEN

We have terrible senses of direction and neither of has learned how to turn the ignition to leave our bodies behind. So we walk, but never in a straight line. You blame your poor balance on being born premature; I blame mine on alcoholism. But I often think we are saying the same thing.

I say, *this life is tightrope* and you hand me a balancing pole, which is really a tube of black cherry lipstick, sometimes liquid eyeliner. I tell you, *my guilty pleasure is Tudor style homes and I think it's because I'm afraid to be made of just one thing.* You know me well enough to know what hurts and where.

Queer, what you have in your hair is all down feathers, dandelion stems, and the ways in which you've saved me. When we take new names, we give each other permission. Call it *cell division.* Call it *asexual reproduction.* Call it *we sexier now.* I say *I want to turn my body into a straight line.*

And you chant until it's true: *Kayla / Kayleb / Chris / Kit.*
You ask, *have you practiced yourself in cursive?*
Have you touched yourself yet in ink?

We allow greed when we are together, because greed, to us, is the only way to stay alive. When I can't see, your name bobby pins the hair from my eyes. When I can't taste, I take the lipstick off your lips with my lips. If imitation is the highest form of flattery, mimicry is me saying, *I love you. I am you.*

ELEGY FOR THE UNDEAD

I admire your half-
life, the way you refuse

complete death and rewrite
your worst misgivings

to be even bloodier.
Beauty is a dead-

dry tongue hollowing
a pulsing conch.

The ocean can be heard
in all empty things.

And it is this quiet wave
sound that explains

the over-confident
swimmer, twist

broke in the rip
tide. Young people die

because they are too alive.
This is proven algorithm.

This is breaststroke
with a concaved lung.

There is a lesson
to be learned

from those that refuse
to go gently. I've learned

to keep my tongue
wet, and soft,

and gentle.

MAKING THE DESERT WET

Before Christ what was there except dissonance, red ridges, and bison run in rhythm with one another? Because I am always lost, I tuck a vision of the last millennia into my breast pocket and it smokes up like black sand— the Pharaohs Horses crushing my clavicle with bass heavy hooves.

I'm always high on pesticides and saber tooth tigers because time isn't linear and death is one of the saints I pray to. If I were asked to say one true thing, I'd hold my breath through the ages. When I turn blue in the face, the desert becomes an ocean and I want you to imagine the cool insides of an abandoned conch shell. Run your fingers in and out of the smoothness and know my sex is just another illusion. Everything you thought you knew about me: mirage, and the tide all pulled back.

DROUGHT BECOMES ME

What if this Father's Day we all sit quietly and remember the devastation
of biblical fire. Arson is only named arson if it was a man's will to name

it so. When a home burns I can only think of the small explosions
that make the whole. Under the sink aerosol cans swell like God's

broken Sun & the flair of chemical burns can be glamorous & gay
if you are desperate to feel beautiful. I would like to feel beautiful.

My desire cannot be shallow if there is no water to measure.

One day I'll write a poem with no water at all.
And then, how   will we stop this burn.

POEM WITH NO WATER AT ALL

You don't even have to look to know this world smells of lava
and the ways in which we've burnt it. The argument against heat

is a scarecrow smoldering from the inside out. The fields
are locust wing dry and there is little hope if you are listening

carefully to the wind. Most mornings, the day opens its mouth
to spit dust and halfhearted salutations. I do not blame the earth

for its general fatigue but rather embrace the luke-warm
air we walk through. I understand the cough that comes

after finishing a carton. The saddest thing about humans
and the earth is sometimes we smoke

                              when we don't want to.
                              Sometimes we let it all in.

ON ATTEMPTING TO CLEAR THE AIR

I am interested in my lungs
mainly because I have never seen them.

Their walls must be mud dark by now.
But finally, I regret every cruelty

I have ever done
unto myself.

This new way of loving
my body has made me

weak with pleasure. I am coming
into my own.

In America, the face of ecstasy
earns an R rating and it's true,

my face is appropriate
                              for nothing.

You don't even have to
look to know.

I WISH ALL CHILDREN COULD TOUCH THE SKY AT LEAST ONCE

The American West is burning
and young boys take

this opportunity to experiment
with bottle rockets, make metaphors

of their newly lit violence.
They want to know

how dangerous they can become
if they work hard at destruction,

and acres is the answer.
We all want to hate these boys

but instead settle
to hate their flammable

fathers—those raised fists, those holes
in the drywall. On the other side

of the country, a rainbow falls
complete over my house.

My niece, just two years old,
whispers *roy gee biv*

for the first time, then weeps
as all that color sinks

back into the storm.
The most beautiful

things are temporary.
She knows this now.

She knows this before
she knows much else.

FOURTH OF JULY AND TRANS ON THE BROOKLYN SIDE

Smoke tails of fireworks trail and the little boy
next to me muses on the origin of everything.

He wonders aloud if the *fire booms* live in the river
they're shot from or in the clouds they light up.

And that, I think, is the best question I've ever heard.
Origin is cumulous. Origin is Hudson River murky.

The boy's father gives everything to god and god
gives back. He says to his son, *God is raining*

glitter from his palms. He says *Jesus is a jellyfish*
that flies; he lights up like your new shoes.

And, really, what is faith if not
imaginative? Religion if not vibrant?

This Father, this Son, this Holy Ghost of fire
working through the sky, they compel me.

So when the boy asks me what I am,
I understand the question and answer,

glitter glue, pipe cleaner, red white and blue
rocket pop, a jellyfish under blacklight.

The boy looks into me.
He gives me to God.

ON FIRST MEETING MY FUTURE HUSBAND-WIFE
(OR, WHEN THE AQUARIANS DECLARE AFFECTION
AND INTENTIONS TO DISMANTLE GENDER)

In 48 hours I say hello and goodbye so many times
my tongue rolls like hard candies spilled

from a blue glass bowl. One day soon I will give you a ring
made exclusively of my white hairs. There are ways

to make knots new: something home grown,
stratus clouds, a prayer and a mantis walking—

stilt legs stippling the water. When we boil ourselves
down to the base, gravity is heavy love and

every poem is really a poem about aging, counting
seconds as stars, or as skips of a rock

along what mirages silken. We were born
under the same sun sign, and can I ask you

what hemisphere looks up our skirts
on the first day of spring? Can I ask

if this is where we keep secrets for one another?
Little water bearers. What if we spill

and break all this celestial balance?

what is distance besides finding horse faces in the clouds and knowing you can see them too. omniscient is my head in the sky. omniscient is my nipples hardening because there's always an ice storm this high up and i can see you from here. omniscient is sometimes the enemy and my grandfather's favorite book was *the old man and the sea.* my mother told me that was all about loneliness. and because i'm scared to be lonely and you find hemingway boring, i'd rather watch you sail. i know you'd stitch your body into a bright flag. i know you'd wolf-bite your nails into paddles and poseidon would gossip to his sirens that he's never seen anyone quite like you. i know you'd turn your face to the sky and i would tell you everything; i'd say: when you chap from sea salt i'll turn my mouth into a faucet and rain for you. when you say glory, i'll say amen and finger fuck the clouds, weather wrapped in my palms as gift. when you ask the distance between you and me: costal, tidal, a grotto filled to brim with the way it feels to touch someone new.

WHEN VESUVIUS ERUPTS AGAIN I'LL COOL MY TONGUE IN THE MEDITERRANEAN (OR, I THINK OUR BODIES ARE BOTH MOLTEN AND MOLTING)

if an orgasm is always a volcano, every volcano is my name. Lover Boy, when i see you in the bushes, you are the blood i want to swallow; your feathers paint my mouth with revlon. you call me *cherry noble* when my lipstick flumes up red rock. you laugh when i can't confirm god is a woman simply because i'm not so sure i am. catholicism is as bankrupt as blockbuster so us queers are bent on rebranding. and Cover Girl, when my great grandfather fought on the beaches of normandy the bullets thumped fire through the sand. everyone was walking on broken glass, ash, boney ember. the largest amphibious assault ever recorded, and i think of the geckos i chased in florida—their feet paddling the white sand. their tails bouquets of cold blood in my hand. you should know i look nothing like my maternal family. i am mediterranean and when i fall in love it's a magmatic mushroom cloud. i want to tell you *every forget-me-not is really a scar* so i hope you believe everything i say. an honest disguise isn't a disguise at all.

LOVE POEM WRITTEN FOR THE LAST SWAMPLAND
(OR, GLOBAL WARMING MAKES US FUCK DESPERATELY)

the flamingo's neck as shotgun barrel—yes i'm cocked constant for you. kink sweetly all over my back and know between my legs is twink canyon and   nail polish removed. raw is nailing me to our bed. what's gone is what was never meant to be. so when you say, *water flatters the summer*, do you mean my sweat smells of turpentine, lily pads, and the end of the earth? when you measure me, wingspan is ruled by tongue, height encompassed by your cardinal throat. directionless, i say *go south* and imitate flowers in the passenger seat: the shrug of lilacs, the last curtsy of a wild flower coughing up typhoid. if you're ever fevering, i'll LL cool J lick my lips around you, because it can be dry in the final june, and there will be no saxophone attending the apocalypse. the reeds are dried blood and cackle when fire comes. you say, *i'll touch you while the world burns.* you name my clit *cock.* you put me in your hands; you trigger pull; you suggest we colt python and free range the day away.

WHEN THE SISSIES MAKE LOVE TO EVERY CARDINAL DIRECTION

you dream of cockpits and i am all bad puns, innuendos, and admitting i've fallen in love with you. so let's fly somewhere. this is another love poem. count your flamingos on one hand, raise a leg and point west. i know you want cactus spines in your palm, a desert on your tongue, and I'm a strip club glitter highway, so touch me to be dirty and lit on light. glitter between molars grinds the same grain as glass. blue bottles pounded down by the tide, my teeth are gnash-rare, and attempt to be the sea on your skin. when i tell you i love you it spills out as *all light floats.* you appreciate the concept and say you want the shape the sun, put your hands around its neck and squeeze until it moan-chokes a solar flare. because i'm light and want to be bent, i come again and again as star dust/&/lightning struck emoji. you say *everything is a circle under the surface* and i regurgitate like a bird. *everything is a circle under the surface, which is to say, an earthworm has a core, and the earth has five hearts.* i am making my body earth, and when i do, how many hearts can i hand you? how many beats until we hit bass, and i let you see the bottom?

CLEOPATRA CAME OUT AS QUEER BUT THE WORLD WAS NOT QUITE READY (OR, MY FUTURE HUSBAND-WIFE COMPLETES A RUBIK PYRAMID IN SECONDS SO THERE IS STILL HOPE IN THIS WORLD FOR US WHO ARE LIVING)

The wind feels breezy
and apocalyptic.

So, machete my jungle
wet mouth to bits and understand

Cleopatra did many things
worth loving.

She said *snakebite* and
the world swung

a jump rope around the sexed-
split tongue of the Nile.

I'll admit that I want to be
both queer

and immeasurably powerful.
These are cosmically meant

to coexist. At night, my partner
uses their angel-

sharp fingers to clean
my wounds, plucks

tendons like chord progressions.
We keep cobra

venom in our pockets.
We love

each other unexplainable,
like which came first,

the chicken
or the egg.

We love each other
like queers immortal.

WHEN CLEOPATRA COMES BACK FROM THE DEAD SHE ASKS ME
TO EXPLAIN KINK, LOVE, AND MY TRANSGENDER BODY

So I tell her:
          My kink is butter milk and my partner begging
me to *please forget your father*. My partner has named my thighs
beachside and the receding gulf of muscle memory.

Here, I enjoy a world in which I am half water
and half the sand to keep it in—half man,
half woman just learning to swim.

Cleopatra is confused by both my body
and the washing machine. I explain whirlpool
is just the Kraken opening its mouth and trying
to siren-sing to its lover locked on land.

Language is barrier only if the water churns
counter clockwise. Cleopatra mentions Caesar
obliquely and I say, *He was no good for you.*
There is always time to make something new.

IF JULIET AND JULIET CHANGE THEIR NAMES TO ROMEO AND ROMEO DOES EVERYONE STILL DIE? (OR, THE THEORY OF OPPOSITES IS BEST EXPLAINED BY A MIRROR)

A nuclear power plant flumes the wide hips of lady liberty. So the inside of my nose is oxidized and if I do one good thing in this life it's kick every bottoms up penny. There is luck in tossing back a shot of sleep. Power is poison for another, or maybe power is in dying for yourself. Do you think Romeo's last drink was green? Do you think it slicked Juliet's throat like the lube I like most?

You know, let's all just tingle into darkness
and understand something about ourselves.

In my dreams, I swim in polluted water. I wake up amalgamate monster. I wake up man. Juliet tells me *opposite is the need.* And I know she is telling me to kneel and take her cock in my mouth. She says *there is grace in being both burial and a battery charge, sin in being both dead and alive.* She says *bottoms tilt their heads up and open their eyes.*

Romeo shouts from a mahogany coffin that his body
is a betrayal—always has been.

My hands are pistols. My cunt keeps writing poems. America is a phallus and lady liberty is rotting green in the sun. If I am Juliet, then Romeo, let me take your sunburn down to a simmer. Let me slice open what I know of myself. Aloe is copper in the water and I just want to be cool.

I IMAGINE JULIET AND SNOW WHITE WOULD MAKE A BEAUTIFUL COUPLE AND I WOULD WATCH THEM KISS WITHOUT A QUESTION (OR, BEING AWAKE MAKES IT MUCH EASIER TO REALIZE YOURSELF)

Romeo is finally dead. And I wonder, can I love two women together if I no longer am one? I've got a new name and my teeth slide out of my mouth in my dreams—

terra cotta tiles tumbled off my dead grandfather's roof. To me, baking soda is toothpaste and drugs. My gums bleed white red froth. To me, gender is killing.

Listen: I want to look at women, keep my gaze undetectable. Someone please stop me. Lineage: my grandfather gets pulled over drunk, vodka in the cup

holder, cocaine white inside white sock inside boot. Hardly ever a repercussion if you powder your white man nose to snow, keep your hand on the clutch, keep your breath

hung white in cold air. When I get caught stealing the storeowner lets me keep my pockets full but calls me a *pretty little girl* and brushes his fingertips across the nipples that peak

mountainous beneath my shirt. Most things have a price for some people. I would balance my checkbook if I knew how. When I was young my father called me his daughter

but spoke about women as though I were his son. I remember how heavy his hands fell when they patted my back. Now my partner dreams they are in a field of waist high hay—

the sky a painful blue. There is no water or ocean or lake but they are still building a life-boat. And isn't that the most beautiful thing? To want to survive even your sleep?

Isn't it terrible to know you must?

POEM IN WHICH I DREAM SHARE WITH MY FUTURE HUSBAND-WIFE (OR, "SHARING ALL" IS A STATEMENT IN ABSOLUTE)

At night you keep your head inside the corona
of my past life and you are brave to invite

yourself into such an unsafe house. I lived
so lonely there. In this dream, which is also

my dream, you bleed onto a plywood floor.
When you clean the mess, you splinter

yourself to bits. My mother may or may
not hurt or help the way your blood

falls. You feel the walls walk in
and so you walk out. Escape

to the forest but the forest
is everywhere. The forest is made

of marble. The forest is a séance-
ring of Apollo's head, Grandpappy's

grave, gargoyle poised for angry
flight, sundial in the dead of night.

You say, *The snow was falling thick.*
I could feel your father above me. You say,

Kayleb, he may have been the snow.

SOMEDAY I'LL LOVE MYSELF SEE THROUGH

My doppelganger must be female bodied
because y'all keep calling my uterus

a mansion. Revise: I want to cut you
and your calfskin. My family has roots

in meat packing. And my hips are so wide
my children must be, will be, need me

gorgeous; won't they? But I am only an em
dash—nothing can fit itself inside a line

but a boy who needs attention. Cellophane
is see through. My chest: leftovers,

and milk spoiled in the fridge. My mother
doesn't like calling me by a boy's name.

But she does it. *Wrap yourself*
tighter, Kayleb. Everyone sees through.

The boy inside needs a womb.

A LIMBO MOON ABOVE // YOU WILL FALL IN LIMBO LOVE

Truly, there is nothing bigger than my boyhood,
the way it blooms big from cock and the nuclear
waste river my parents swam through as children.

I once read that metamorphosis dictates point A
and point B, but names the in-between the first
ring of hell. Fag limbo is my body inside another

body, between the thighs of my partner's holiest
body. Fag limbo is my mother forbidding I dance
the Macarena but teaching my hips to write cursive

Ss and rattle snakes in the silt. Here are some
rings in order: limbo, birch tree, and the chainsaw
to fell it, cut diamond, fire, and lies to melt it.

//

There is nothing more powerful than my mouth
and who I choose to let live there. At night, when I speak
with God, I say *Gluttony strokes the queer to joy. And Honey,*
                                        we like it that way.

OUR ROOT SYSTEM IS A TANGLE OF PIPECLEANERS
(OR, BEING YOUR MAN HAS MADE ME ONE)

I'd love to huff cedar stain
and tell you how I love you,

but woodworking is how my father
loved my mother and I'd like to forget

this fact and build something wholly new.
So, if the mountains pray to peaches

then my skin must bruise like a starry night. I'll teach
you to fight, if you love my Appalachian roots

and keep your tongue in my ear. You lick my wounds
and yours, and we are both healing faster than ever, aren't we?

For you, I am on my knees breezing saints into the sand. For you,
I want to be married on a Jersey beach and learn to swim.

All the gay saints will be in attendance. When we come out
to each other we whisper vows to one another's tiny cocks

before bed. Asparagus is sequoia strong
if you believe in rooting for the underdog.

Together, we have no time
to be anything less than large.

MY HOROSCOPE IS MY FUTURE HUSBAND'S HOROSCOPE & WE ARE BOTH CHANGING SO QUICKLY

After Jennifer Jackson Berry
And after Hernan Bas's *River Crossing*

With the Sun spotlighting our house
of family, it is time to send down
roots & seek belonging.

& belonging is the song
that plays between our legs
when our legs tangle, isn't it?

Spring is the season to collect
ourselves—to fill our well

with something valuable, vial
of our blood oaths & perhaps

marriage. *Only strong relationships*
will survive & I refuse

metaphor only when fact
is more beautiful.

Fact:

        I will hold your hand
        & I will hold your hand steady.

Husband, nothing is holy
like self-construction.

Our fathers built staircases & we are bringing
sledgehammers to our bodies so gently
only we can hear this pleasure.

There is nowhere to go
but into one another.

We will be careful not to burn
the candle at both ends.

MY FUTURE HUSBAND-WIFE AND I MAKE A BLOOD PACT
TO BECOME THE FATHERS WE ALWAYS NEEDED

Because we want our future
children alive

with the fire
of no abuse

we shake
each other

by the hand and by the body
in a contract that will last

as long as we are living.
We expel from our veins

the blood our fathers
put there—

but it is slow
going, to excavate

all these paternal lines.
In the meantime,

please show us one gentle
father, and perhaps we will believe

such a thing
exists, and that we can become so.

Our imaginary children already make us
do all sorts of things

that we feel proud of. See,
already, less blood,

so gentle.

LOVE POEM WITH A LACK OF CONCEPTION

In our raunchy love
we ache for household—

welcome mat, shoes strewn
or orderly, a kitchen

made of granite and cutting
blocks. We finger fuck

cumulous clouds
and yearn for a home

and a mortgage and a child.
How many times have we tried

to become
pregnant

during a storm of our sameness?
When we bleed it betrays

us in every way a color can.
I take off your shoes.

I clean you. We lay down
in no home
            in particular.

THOUGHTS ON ROMANCE AS THE HEAT INDEX RISES

I open my mouth and, despite the world,
use it almost daily to fall in love.

This is so direly human of me—
so egregiously alive. I feel

lucky to hold my partner's skin
and their hunger on my tongue

always. I am thankful that, most
mornings, the day still opens

its mouth
for both of us.

NOTES TOWARD TOP SURGERY AND THE IMPENDING
DEATH OF THE BARRIER REEF

//

When my breasts are finally removed
I imagine they will be made
into mountains   elsewhere.

A popular hiking destination,
the boys will hold
what used to be my body

up, and on a pedestal,

or perhaps

        they will climb
        until something structural
        breaks, and the mountain

plateaus into just
an average, flat,
topography.

\\

//

In this life, fire lives
    in the water
        rent free and swan
            boats are the last
            viable mode of transportation.

        Romance in the new millenniaa
    two trans boys   kissing
                    as bird necks wrap
                    their wrists
                    too tight.

My partner talks about my top
surgery like I have never
even considered true   stillness.

    They talk about bed   rest
    on a salt water raft—   floating
    with no oars   for months.

How thirsty can two boys on a raft

become? They say,   *you will not*
turn   *crescents into*   *blood*

moons with blown stiches.
They say, *you will never be the same.*

    Isn't that something.

\\

//

As a child I read and reread
the story of a girl who wore a forest
green ribbon round her neck for a lifetime.

And as she lay dying, the ribbon
was untied, her head hit the floor,
the forest was slashed and burned.

At her funeral everyone was talking
about the benefits of deforestation,
and guillotines.

What is a whole life of denying
the truth of your body's
shape? If I am used to wrapping

my chest in an ace bandage,
does that mean I've always
been bleeding?

\\

//

Everyone in America speaks fluid laceration,
with their diamond studded
tongues. Oral sex

is the new corn field
tilled until death do us part.
God, agriculture is so violent,

and I have lusted toward blood-rust:
the hoe, the scalpel, a sharp rake,
and a rototiller pushed across

my mammary glands. Milk as miracle
grow. God, I wish I could touch
myself with any tenderness, any soft,
human, tool.

\\

//

They say anesthesia
is an ocean
of calm,   until
oil hits   the water.
Intubation   is an anchor
                  until
                  it's snagged
                  on the ocean floor.

Complications of double
mastectomies include:
clogged coral, burst arteries,
death. But already when pelicans
open their mouths   the world
                           only remembers
                           how to say

pothole and point
a swollen finger
anywhere but   inward.
                      It is true,

the reef
is almost dead.
But I   am   almost
not.

\\

x

A SPELL TO ABSOLVE YOUR OWN TRANSNESS

start by recognizing the gazelle
of your body

then find the quicksand that lives
between your legs

and the grasslands.
search this sunken field

with your hoof
like fingers,

then craft it a rhinestoned
tiara. forgive that old crown

of thorns but still
shove it down

the garbage disposal.
this world has taught you

the lesson of laceration
quite enough.

and your body deserves
to be unbarbed.

tell it so.

DURING MY TOP SURGERY CONSULTATION, MY PARTNER SAYS TO THE DOCTOR, *TELL ME WHAT YOU WILL DO TO THEIR VEINS*

and no answer will satisfy true
blood flow or this boy who loves me.

The truth is, as I sleep, everything directly above
my heart will be cauterized.

Facts are difficult
if you are able to recognize them

as fact. And I am scared
of my partner

being faced with my blood
because I love them.

When we talk of the future, my future chest is as flat
as our future backyard. We plant

a lemon tree and it grows
even in winter.

MY MOTHER BELIEVES IN MY MARRIAGE AND THIS SHOWS ME
HER HEART CAN FORGIVE EVEN YEARS SPENT DANCING ALONE

When I ask my mother to tell me
a story, she tells me of her cold feet
boiled down in a vat of frogs.

She tells me of the way she danced
romantic with a mop at her wedding
rehearsal. If you ask her, she'll say

the mop had thick Sicilian curls, more
rhythm than my father, and always took out
the trash. She'll say, *I should have thrown*

my body
            in reverse, killed
                        the headlights, and hid.

She'll say, *you have his hair,*
and when your eyes flash red
I see him and a turn
signal onto a back road.

It is true that

                    I want to spend   my life apologizing
                    for both my body   and my anger,
                    but neither have   killed anyone yet.

This is a triumph of blood.
This is a u-turn. In my family,
moving backward is progress.

In my family, water boils
to ice, and songs sound better
while rewound. When I tell

my mother I've met the man
I want to marry she asks
to give me away.

EXPRESSING MY FEELINGS TO MY FUTURE HUSBAND-WIFE (OR, RITUAL IN WHICH GENDER)

//

Just out of high school
I worked as a statue

of liberty. I wore blue velvet
and danced along an off

shoot of route 6. Mascot
for freedom—I advertised

a tax agency. I had come
out that year.

Passersby rolled
down their windows,

threw lit cigarettes, trash, pennies.
I have always been one for retaliation.

So I threw the torch.

\\

//

My partner and I research the back-
yard tree with purple droppings

until we discover
the tree's a true princess.

Royal green blood with roots the
size of bodies.

This princess is invasive.
She garden snakes under

our home and upheaves what
we thought we knew

of ourselves. And god, isn't
it terrible to gender

even a tree. Isn't it terrible that
she reminds us of what

we've named our bodies'
shortcomings. A flower

concaved as cunt
seems, right now, like a betrayal we

will never forgive.

But soon

\\

//

I dream that my partner leaves
me for eight years in the Coast Guard,

a kraken stings the surface
of this dark blue nightmare.

Split this dream in half and it becomes
four years and I still don't know

how to swim. None of this is real.
But god, my partner loves the water,

enough even, for me to get in.

\\

//

When my partner turns their hands
into window blinds, they smooth

my aging forehead with this new
type of shade. They call my skin

into perfect order with their skin.

I tell my partner I will be polite
to windows

only when I like what I see
through them. They understand

that this world is hell
bent beyond repair.

But inside
           one another
           there is a peace.

Inside one another
neither of us remembers gender—the meaning
of her or hers. She is lost
                to space. He was never
                that great to begin with.

We even misplaced the meaning of girl.

If we knew where it had been left,
we still wouldn't go get it.

**

//

Today I am the age
of an arsenal
                of letters.

Between my partner's legs
I speak the whole

alphabet. They stop me

when I'm close
to what feels right.

At the end of the day
all we have is this ritual

of love, and that, I think,
will be enough

to live forever.

\\

IN BED WITH MY FUTURE

Husband, we have yet to learn
so many things. Can you feel

the beauty of our unknowing?
When I tell you that removing parts

of my body is preservation
of the last rainforest,

you say: *something always
has to die for the rest to live.*

You pack
so much acceptance

into your pants, that I am overwhelmed
by your goodness.

We will spend
half our lives

in bed together. There, I take the heat
off your back

with my mouth and feel rough
fevers of affection.

Husband, you kiss my upper lip
when it's shaved
                    and when it isn't.

You kiss the head of my cock
as it bleeds.

I kiss your blood
right back.

What a simple and complete
way to love.

END

NOTES

All the Gay Saints began as an extended exercise in ekphrasis. Many poems are in direct conversation with the paintings of Hernan Bas. The poems that owe creative debt to Bas are listed below, alongside their corresponding painting titles. I encourage all to spend some time with Bas' work.

"When I transition will I lose my taste for the storm?"
// After Hernan Bas' *a landscape to swallow you whole*

"If the water weren't so deep, Narcissus might not have drowned (Or, when coming out as trans to my younger self)"
// After Hernan Bas' *the primordial soup theory (homosexual)*

"Comforting my trans self through the night (Or, on dreaming my breasts are removed only to grow back—again and again)"
// After Hernan Bas' *Red Herring*

"Making the Desert Wet"
// After Hernan Bas' *Laocoôn Sons*

"Funeral for a girl who grew up in the woods (Or, at the root)"
// After Hernan Bas' *At the root of his thinking (or the pink blossom)*

"On First Meeting my Future Husband-Wife (Or, when the Aquarians Declare Affection)"
// After Hernan Bas' *Wine River (fountain of youth)*

"a night on the town with my future husband-wife"
// After Hernan Bas' *Downhill at Dusk (the Runaway)*

"1081 nautical miles and i want to ask you"
// After Hernan Bas' *The Giant's Watering Hole*

"When Vesuvius Erupts Again I'll Cool my Tongue in the Mediterranean (Or, I think our bodies are both molten and molting)"
// After Hernan Bas's *Vesuvius*

"love poem written for the last swampland (or, global warming makes us fuck desperately)"
// After Hernan Bas's *The Floridian*

"When the sissies make love to every cardinal direction"
// After Hernan Bas' *The Softspoken Sissy with Spoonbill Feathers*

"When Cleopatra comes back from the dead she asks me to explain kink, love, and my transgender body"
// After Hernan Bas' *Tantalus*

"a limbo moon above // you will fall in limbo love"
// After Hernan Bas' *His voice would be the loudest in the land*

"Our root system is a tangle of pipecleaners (Or, being your man has made me one)"
// After Hernan Bas's *The Horn of Plenty*

"There is a point at which i tire of my own fear"
// After Hernan Bas' *Unknown Poet #24 (Not Afraid of the Dark)*

"Sinners must live with what their sins sow"
// After Hernan Bas' *The Garden Always Looked Different at Night*

"my shadow looks more like a man than i do, so i am both fearful and envious"
// After Hernan Bas' *Tracing Shadoes (or The Mistaken silhouette)*

"Someday I'll love myself see through"
// After Hernan Bas' *The Burden (I shall leave no memoirs)*

"Poem in which I dream share with my future husband-wife (Or, "sharing all" is a statement in absolute)"
// After Hernan Bas' *A Satanist on a Tuesday (or, The Key Master)*

"my body is constantly conjuring a tempest (or, weighing the pros and cons of attending my high school reunion)"
// After Hernan Bas' *On the Jagged Shores*

"I imagine Juliet and Snow White would make a beautiful couple and I would watch them kiss without a question (Or, being awake makes it much easier to realize yourself)"
// After Hernan Bas' *Hope*

"If Juliet and Juliet change their names to Romeo and Romeo does everyone still die? (Or, the theory of opposites is best explained by a mirror)"
// After Hernan Bas' *In the future, crystals will mean everything*

"a spell to absolve your own transness"
// After Hernan Bas' *Saint Sebastian (arrows for martyrs)*

"Notes Toward Top Surgery and the Impending Death of the Barrier Reef"
// After Hernan Bas' *The Great Barrier Wreath*

"Elegy for the Undead"
// After Hernan Bas' *Night of the Living Dead Gorgeous*

"My horoscope is my future husband's horoscope & we are both changing so quickly"
// After Hernan Bas' *River Crossing*

"My mother believes in my marriage and this shows me her heart can forgive even years spent dancing alone"
// After Hernan Bas' *Leaving the Nest*

"On wanting top surgery in the fascist regime" adapts the language of Walt Whitman's "I sing the body electric."

"Someday I'll love myself see through" is written in a linage and after Ocean Vuong, Rodger Reeves, and Frank O'Hara.

"My horoscope is my future husband's horoscope & we are both changing so quickly" is after Jennifer Jackson Berry's "Fat Girl Reads Her Horoscope" and lifts lines from Café Astrology's Aquarius monthly horoscope—April, 2017.

And finally, an immense creative debt to my partner, who's voice and imagination fuels many poems, but particularly: "When Vesuvius Erupts Again I'll Cool my Tongue in the Mediterranean (Or, I think our bodies are both molten and molting)"; "love poem written for the last swampland (or, global warming makes us fuck desperately)"; "When the sissies make love to every cardinal direction"; "When Cleopatra Comes Back from the Dead She Asks Me to Explain Kink, Love, and my Transgender Body"; "Poem in Which I Dream Share with my Future Husband-Wife (Or, "sharing all" is a statement in absolute)"; "Notes Toward Top Surgery and the Impending Death of the Barrier Reef"; and "In Bed with My Future."

ACKNOWLEDGEMENTS

I owe immense debt of gratitude to the journals in which these poems first appeared, sometimes in different forms. Thank you, thank you.

Adroit: "My mother believes in marriage and this shows me her heart"

Blueshift Journal: "my body is constantly conjuring a tempest"

Boaat Press: "I imagine Juliet and Snow White would make a beautiful couple," and "If Juliet and Juliet change their names to Romeo and Romeo"

Boston Review: "Poem with No Water at All"

Cosmonauts Avenue: "on trespassing"

Cream City Review: "love poem written for the last swampland," and "When Vesuvius Erupts Again I'll cool my tongue in the Mediterranean"

Dreginald: "Cleopatra came out as queer but the world was not quite ready," "Elegy for the Undead," "On Harvesting Oneself," and "The Once Girl Hunts to Feed"

Grist: "My horoscope is my future husband's horoscope & we are both changing so quickly," "my shadow looks more like a man than i do," and "Sinners must live with what their sins sow"

Hayden's Ferry Review and Academy of American Poets: "Expressing my feelings to my future husband-wife (or, ritual in which gender)"

Interrupture: "1081 nautical miles and i want to ask you," and "Thoughts on Romance as the Heat Index Rises"

Lambda Literary Fellows Anthology: "On First Meeting my Future Husband-Wife"

Mondegreen: "Comforting my trans self through the night" (as "The first Nocturne")

Muzzle, Best of the Net, and *Bettering American Poetry*: "Fourth of July and Trans on the Brooklyn Side"

Pen American, The Rattling Wall, Election Protest Anthology: "When Face to Face with Fascism" (as "There is so much country for old men, so")

Pittsburgh Poetry Review: "Our Root System is a Tangle of Pipecleaners," "When Cleopatra comes back from the dead," and "When I transition will I lose my taste for the storm?"

Platypus Press, A Portrait in Blues Anthology: "On wanting top surgery in the fascist regime"

Rabbit Catastrophe: "a spell to absolve your own transness"

Radar Poetry: "Someday I'll love myself see through," and "Poem in which I dream share with my future husband-wife"

RHINO: "Making the desert wet"

Sixth Finch: "a limbo moon above // you will fall in limbo love"

Sonora Review: "If the water weren't so deep, Narcissus might not have drowned"

storySouth: "When the sissies make love to every cardinal direction"

The Tiny: "there is a point at which i tire of my own fear," "My future husband-wife and I make a blood pact to become the fathers we always needed," and "On Attempting to Clear the Air"

Timber: "Love Poem with a Lack of Conception"

Tinderbox:" "During my top surgery consultation, my partner says to the doctor, *tell me what you will do to their veins,*" "Funeral for a Girl who Grew Up in the Woods" and "Two Queers Walking the Borderline Between"

TriQuarterly: "Notes toward top surgery and the impending death of the barrier reef"

Thank you to Henry Israeli, Christopher Salerno, Rebecca Lauren, Robin Vuchnich, Jake Bauer, and the whole Saturnalia Books team. I am forever grateful to be part of the Saturnalia family.

I am endlessly thankful to be alive and writing with my peers. What a beautiful time this is for poems.

Thank you to Natalie Diaz for supporting this work and helping me make it better. And thank you to T Fleischmann for being so generous with your words and time.

Thank you to the amazing Tomas Harker, whose 2016 painting, *Nocturne,* is on the cover of this book. And thank you to Hernan Bas, for the paintings that inspired many of these poems, and a whole new way to see my body in the forest.

Thank you to my teachers, Julia Kasdorf, TC Tolbert, L. Lamar Wilson, Wendy Rawlings, and Michael Martone, for always lending your time and energy.

Thank you to Rachel Franklin Wood, Stephanie Trott, Kasey Clark, Despy Boutris, Rachel Cruea, and Avren Keating, for taking the time to ask me about my work. I value those conversations more than y'all may know.

Thank you to the Whiting Foundation and the support of the Lambda Literary Retreat. A special shout out to Harry's Smokeshop in Philadelphia and Egans Bar in Tuscaloosa. My second homes.

All light and love to my beautiful friends, who support me and my work at every turn: Joshua Sanders, Kit Emslie, Reem Abu-Baker, Shelley Feller, Diamond Forde, Nabila Lovelace, C. Russell Price, Shaelyn Smith, Marina Oney, Anna Ladd, Brian Oliu, Berry Grass, Laura Kochman, Ever Sugarman, Jenifer Park, MK Foster, Hannah Rubin, RB Brown, Geoffrey Emerson, Julia Coursey, Rachel Brown, Rachel Dispenza, Grant TerBush and all my other generous and kind buddies. Life wouldn't be half as sweet without you.

Gratitude beyond words to all who made my top surgery possible.

Thank you to my family, who is supportive of all I do. Specifically, thank you Momma Bear, Grandmommy, Kimmy, Nana, and Victoria. You all mean the world to me.

And lastly, thank you to Jack Papanier, my partner in this life, and if I'm lucky, the next too. Thank you for this love. I can't wait to bring it everywhere we go. All light floats, Jack. I'm yours through the storm.

ABOUT THE AUTHOR

Kayleb Rae Candrilli is a 2019 Whiting Award Winner in Poetry and the author of *What Runs Over* with YesYes Books, which was a 2017 finalist for the Lambda Literary Award in transgender poetry. *All the Gay Saints* is their second collection and won the 2018 Saturnalia Book Contest. Candrilli's third collection, *Water I Won't Touch,* is forthcoming from Copper Canyon Press. Their work is published in *POETRY, American Poetry Review, Boston Review,* and many others. They live in Philadelphia with their partner.

Also by Kayleb Rae Candrilli:

What Runs Over
YesYes Books, 2017

All the Gay Saints is printed in Adobe Garamond Pro.

www.saturnaliabooks.org